Sports Illustrated KIDS

BIG BOOK OF WHO

WOMEN IN SPORTS

Library of Congress Cataloging-in-
Publication Data available upon request.

This book is available in quantity
at special discounts for your
group or organization.

For further information, contact:
Triumph Books LLC
814 North Franklin Street
Chicago, Illinois 60610
(312) 337-0747
www.triumphbooks.com

ISBN 978-1-63727-683-9

Printed in U.S.A.

Cover design by Drew Dzwonkowski
and Preston Pisellini

WOMEN IN SPORTS

▶ Inspirational and aspirational. Fearless and phenomenal. The best women athletes—past and present—are all here! From those who dominated their sport to the ones who broke barriers and paved the way for others to follow, these stories bring excellence in sports to girls and boys alike. This fun collection of questions and answers will have you stumping all the fans in your life!

CONTENTS

These athletes reinvented what it means to be a sports celebrity

SUPER

STARS

Which skier has won the most World Cup crystal globe titles?

Alpine skier **Lindsey Vonn** was born to hit the slopes. She was up on skis by the time she was two years old. By 16, she had made the U.S. Ski Team. She won four World Cup overall championships and was the first American woman to win the gold medal in downhill, at the 2010 Winter Olympics. In 2016, she won her 20th crystal globe, awarded to the skier with the most World Cup points titles in individual disciplines and overall, the most in history. Vonn is one of only six women who has won World Cup races in all five disciplines of alpine skiing—downhill, super-G, giant slalom, slalom, and super combined. Injuries caused Vonn to miss parts of several seasons, and she announced her retirement in 2019.

FAST FACT:
Vonn amassed a total of 82 World Cup victories during her career. Only Mikaela Shiffrin (97) and Ingemar Stenmark (86) have more than Vonn.

Who has been named FIFA World Player of the Year more than anyone?

Some athletes win wherever they go. **Marta** is one of those people. From 2005 through 2015, while playing for clubs in Sweden, Brazil, and the U.S., she led her teams to league championships in every year but one, winning FIFA World Player of the Year five times in a row beginning in 2006, and then a sixth time in 2018. As a striker for Brazil's national team, Marta received the Golden Ball (top player) and Golden Boot (top scorer) at the 2007 World Cup, during which she led Brazil to its first final. She also helped her country win back-to-back silver medals at the 2004 and 2008 Olympics, and was one of eight athletes who carried the Olympic flag at the 2016 Games, which Brazil hosted. Born Marta Vieira da Silva, she has more international goals (122) than fellow Brazilian Péle, who is often called the greatest soccer player of all time.

Which singles player has the most Grand Slam titles of any woman in the Open era?

She won her first Grand Slam event, the 1999 U.S. Open, when she was only 17 years old. By the time her career was over, **Serena Williams** had won more major tournaments (23) than any woman since professionals were first allowed to participate in them, in 1968. To go along with her six victories at the U.S. Open, she has seven at the Australian Open, three at the French Open, and seven at Wimbledon. In 2003 and 2015, she completed what became known as the Serena Slam, winning four major tournaments in a row (a little different than a true Grand Slam, which entails four wins in a calendar year). "I do want to be known as the greatest ever," she said in 2015.

It's hard to argue that she's not. Since first topping the world rankings in 2002, she has been number one for 319 weeks, including 186 in a row.

After she won the 2017 Australian Open—seven matches in straight sets—while pregnant with her daughter, Alexis, Williams ascended to the top spot again. At 35, she was the oldest number one in history.

WOW FACTOR

14

Number of doubles Grand Slams she and her sister, Venus, have won together. They are 14–0.

"The success of every woman should be the inspiration to another. We should raise each other up. Make sure you're very courageous. Be strong, be extremely kind, and above all, be humble."

—in 2015, at the Glamour Women of the Year Awards

Who has won the most beach volleyball tournaments of all time?

She may have begun her career playing indoors, but the 6' 3" **Kerri Walsh Jennings** made her name on the soft sand of the world's beach volleyball courts. A four-time All-America for Stanford's NCAA indoor team, she played for the U.S. at the 2000 Olympics. The next year, she joined Misty May-Treanor on the pro beach international tour (FIVB) and then on the U.S. circuit, the AVP Tour. Together the duo earned six consecutive AVP Team of the Year awards (2003 through 2008), three straight FIVB world championships (2003, 2005, and 2007), and three Olympic gold medals (2004, 2008, 2012).

After May-Treanor retired, Jennings partnered with April Ross; they won 11 of the 32 international tournaments they entered and snagged bronze at the 2016 Olympics. That year, Jennings became the first U.S. woman to win 600 international matches. She's taken first at 133 tournaments, making her the winningest women's beach player in history.

Who beat her famous brother to the basketball Hall of Fame by 17 years?

When she arrived at USC in 1982, **Cheryl Miller** had just led Riverside (California) Polytechnic High to a 132–4 record over four years. She also held state marks for points in a career (3,405) and a season (1,156). And yet, she said at the time, "I don't consider myself a superstar."

When she graduated from USC, there was no doubt in *anyone's* mind just how extraordinary she was: The three-time Naismith Player of the Year and four-time All-America had led the Trojans to two NCAA championships and Team USA to gold at the 1984 Olympics. Miller hustled and she had style, and she grabbed offensive rebounds better than anyone. Younger brother Reggie was no slouch either: He was a five-time All-Star in 18 years with the Indiana Pacers. Cheryl was inducted into the Naismith Memorial Basketball Hall of Fame in 1995; Reggie made it in 2012.

WOW FACTOR

105

Points Miller scored in a game as a high school senior, second-most in history.

FAST FACT:
A four-year starter for the UCLA women's basketball team, she scored 1,167 points and led the Bruins in rebounding as a senior (9.1 per game).

Who has held the world record in the heptathlon since 1988?

To succeed at the heptathlon, a seven-event track and field competition, one needs to be well-rounded. **Jackie Joyner-Kersee** was well-rounded, all right. At the 1988 Olympics, four years after coming in second by a mere five points, she broke her own world record, with 7,291 points, grabbing a gold to add to her silver. (She also won the long jump in 1988, then nabbed bronze in 1992 and 1996.)

At the 1992 Games in Barcelona, Joyner-Kersee didn't match her record. (In 30 years, no one has.) But she did repeat as the gold medalist in the event. She ended her career with two world championships each in the long jump and the heptathlon.

FAST FACT:
Over a nine-year span, Evans went 25–2 in the 400 meters and 22–1 in the 800 at major international competitions.

Which swimmer broke two world records when she was 15 years old?

Before she began her junior year at El Dorado High in California in 1987, 15-year-old freestyle swimmer **Janet Evans** had already finished the 800- and 1,500-meter races faster than anyone in history. That winter, she set the world record in the 400 meters. As a 17-year-old senior, she took the 1988 Olympics by storm, breaking her own world record in the 400 and also winning the 800 meters and the 400 individual medley. (She defended her 800 title in 1992.)

Her best time in the 800 (8:16.22) stood as the world record from 1989 until Rebecca Adlington of Great Britain, who was born in 1989, beat it at the 2008 Games.

Which softball star struck out Major League Baseball sluggers?

A two-time collegiate player of the year, **Jennie Finch** won a record 60 straight games for Arizona, leading the Wildcats to victory at the 2001 Women's College World Series. She was 4–0 in Olympic outings and pitched 19 scoreless innings to help the U.S. win gold at the 2004 Games and silver in 2008. Her pitches reached 70 miles per hour. At the 2004 Pepsi All-Star Softball Game, Finch struck out major leaguers including Albert Pujols and Mike Piazza. "Her fastball was the fastest thing I've ever seen, from that distance," said Brian Giles.

Who was the first female basketball player to get her own signature shoe line?

She was a big enough deal to have a Nike sneaker named after her—and that was before **Sheryl Swoopes** won three Olympic gold medals, three WNBA MVP awards, and four straight WNBA championships with the Houston Comets from 1997 through 2000.

The top girls' high school player in Texas, Swoopes went on to win the 1993 NCAA championship at Texas Tech, where she set eight school records, including the single-game mark for points (53). In 2016, she became the first Red Raider, man or woman, to be inducted into the basketball Hall of Fame.

Which volleyball star was named MVP at the 2020 Tokyo Olympics?

Representing her country at the Olympics has become a quadrennial experience for **Jordan Larson**. An NCAA volleyball champion at Nebraska, Larson was selected as a member of Team USA for the 2016 Games in Rio de Janeiro, the London Games in 2012, and the 2020 Tokyo Olympics. She was captain of the 2020 squad that won gold for the first time in history, scoring 96 points and being named the Most Valuable Player of the event. Larson was also named to the team competing in Paris in 2024.

DID YOU KNOW?

Larson is currently an assistant volleyball coach at Nebraska, which played in front of a record-setting 92,003 fans in August of 2023.

Who is the four-time WNBA champ that led the U.S. to a record five Olympic gold medals?

The NBA has the legendary Larry Bird. The WNBA has the incredible **Sue Bird**. It's hard to choose which one flew higher in their sport. By any measure, Sue Bird is one of the greatest players ever—male or female—to lace up sneakers. After she was the top high school player in her home state of New York, she was the national player of the year with the University of Connecticut in 2002. She joined the Seattle Storm and won the first of her four WNBA titles in 2004. That trophy came after she had led the United States to a gold medal in the 2004 Summer Olympics. She would repeat that feat four more times to become the only person ever with four pro league titles and five Olympic championships in hoops. The great Bird of the WNBA flew into retirement after the 2022 season, knowing someone will have to go a long way to top her marks.

WOW FACTOR

13

The number of WNBA All-Star games that Bird played in during her 19-year career, all with Seattle.

Who was the U.S. Soccer Female Player of the Year five years in a row?

When she was 15, **Mia Hamm** became the youngest person to play for the U.S. national team. When she retired in 2004, she was the organization's all-time leading scorer (158 goals, since passed by Abby Wambach) and was first in the world in international appearances (276, now fourth).

In between, she won two collegiate player of the year awards and helped the University of North Carolina juggernaut win four NCAA titles. She led the country in scoring in 1990, then set the collegiate record for points in a season (97) in 1992.

Hamm played in four World Cups (helping the U.S. win in 1991 and 1999) and three Olympics (leading the U.S. to gold in 1996 and 2004). She was, quite simply, the face of women's soccer in the country when it was gaining momentum in the early 1990s. Hamm earned U.S. Soccer Female Player of the Year honors from 1994 through 1998.

WOW FACTOR

147

Career assists Hamm had in international play, a U.S. record.

FAST FACT:
In 2013, Mia Hamm became the first woman to be inducted into the World Football Hall of Fame in Pachuca, Mexico.

WOW FACTOR

6

Olympic medals Blair won (five gold, one bronze), the most by a female U.S. Winter Olympian.

Which speedskater won the same race in three straight Olympics?

At the 1992 Olympics in Albertville, France, skater **Bonnie Blair** won the 500 meters to become the first woman to win that race at back-to-back Games. She also became the first American Winter Olympian to win consecutive titles in any sport—much to the delight of the 45 family members in the crowd who serenaded her with "My Bonnie Lies Over the Ocean." Blair added gold in the 1,000 that year, then won both events at the next Winter Games, in 1994, ending her career with more golds than any American Winter Olympian. That December, SPORTS ILLUSTRATED named her and fellow speedskater Johann Olav Koss its Sportspeople of the Year.

Who was the first American woman to win an Olympic medal in judo?

She thought she wouldn't make the 2004 Olympics, so high school judoist **Ronda Rousey** named her cat Beijing, the site of the 2008 Games. Well, 17-year-old Rousey made the team in 2004 (she was eliminated early) and again in 2008, winning bronze in the 63-to-70-kg class to become the first American judoist to medal in an Olympics. Over the next decade, she became a Mixed Martial Arts superstar, defending her Ultimate Fighting Championship title six times.

Who shot the lowest round in LPGA tour history?

When she tapped in for par on the 18th hole of her second round at the 2001 Standard Register Ping tournament, **Annika Sorenstam** of Sweden jumped into her caddie's arms. "I'm absolutely overwhelmed," she said. "I can't believe what I just did." That par putt meant she had shot a round of 59, a first on the LPGA tour. Two days later, she set another record by finishing at 27 under par to clinch a victory, one of 72 she racked up over a 15-year career. She won back-to-back U.S. Opens (1995, 1996) and retired with 10 major championship wins, tied with Babe Didrikson Zaharias for fourth-most all time.

At the 2003 Colonial, Sorenstam may not have made the cut, but she became the first woman to play with men on the PGA Tour since Zaharias did it (for the second time) in 1945.

Which member of the Final Five has a gymnastics move named after her?

You know you've made an impact on a sport when you influence the way your fellow athletes train and perform. **Simone Biles** inserted a tumbling pass into her floor exercise routine: a double flip in layout position (straight body) with a half twist and a front landing, which is more difficult than a backward landing. The move was called the Biles, after the woman who perfected it.

If Biles wasn't perfect at the 2016 Olympics, she was close, winning gold in the all-around, floor exercise, and on the vault; earning bronze on the balance beam; and leading the U.S. to gold in the team event.

Her performance at the Games came on the heels of an unprecedented three straight world championships and four consecutive U.S. titles in the all-around.

At the 2020 Tokyo Olympics, Biles was favored to win several medals but withdrew from most of the event after coming down with a case of "the twisties," wherein a gymnast loses awareness of their body in the air. She still won a silver medal with the U.S. team and a bronze medal on the balance beam, and planned to return at the 2024 Games in Paris.

WOW FACTOR

30

World championship medals Biles has won, a record.

23

FAST FACT:
Ladewig was reportedly so fast as a kid that she wasn't allowed to participate in end-of-season races at local playgrounds.

What grandmother of five was named Bowler of the Year a record ninth time in 1963?

In 1955, SPORTS ILLUSTRATED called **Marion Ladewig** "the greatest woman bowler of all time." She had just won five straight U.S. Women's Opens. Her career was far from over, though. She won the tournament three more times and retired with nine Bowler of the Year awards and a record five World's Invitational titles, the last of which she earned in 1965.

A recreational softball player, Ladewig took up bowling when she was 22 only because her friends were into the sport. She put on exhibitions in Europe, Australia, and Asia, and even bowled on the lanes in the White House.

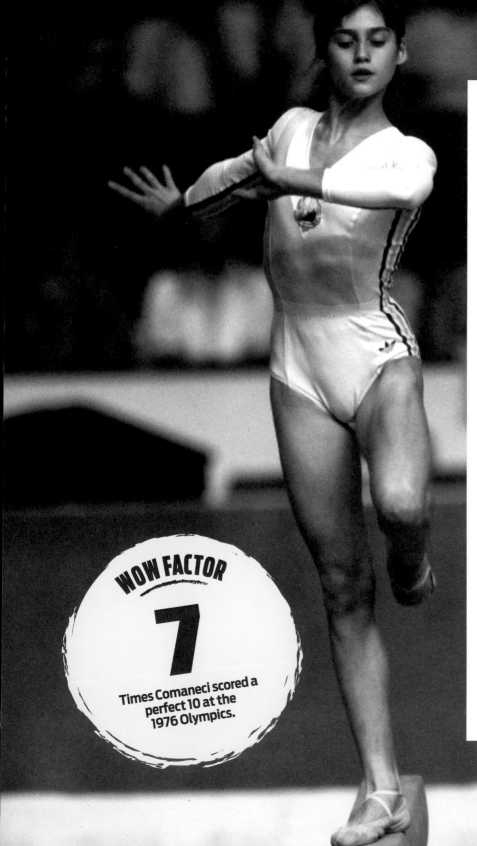

Who was the first gymnast to score a perfect 10?

When <mark>Nadia Comaneci</mark> of Romania finished her uneven bars routine at the 1976 Olympics, she looked up at the scoreboard and saw "1.00." That wasn't how many points she had lost on her routine—the scoreboard just wasn't equipped to display a perfect 10. And for good reason: No gymnast had ever earned one. Not only did she win gold in the uneven bars that year, but she also won the all-around and the beam competition, took silver with her team, and won bronze in the floor exercise. At the 1980 Olympics, she repeated as gold medalist on the balance beam, won another gold for the floor exercise, and also won two silver medals, one for the team all-around and one for individual all-around.

Her coach, Bela Karolyi, went on to mentor future Olympic gold medalists for the U.S. Said Karolyi after Comaneci's performance in 1976, "She has three qualities. The physical qualities—strength, speed, agility. The intellectual qualities—intelligence and the power to concentrate. And . . . Nadia has courage."

WOW FACTOR

7

Times Comaneci scored a perfect 10 at the 1976 Olympics.

Who is the most decorated athlete in U.S. Olympic track and field history?

She lost the 400-meter race at the 2016 Olympics by .07 of a second, but when sprinter **Allyson Felix** stepped off the podium that day with her silver medal, she had collected more Olympic hardware than any American in her sport. As of 2023, she has won gold in the 4 x 400 relay three times and silver once, a gold and two silvers in the 200, a silver and a bronze in the 400, and two golds in the 4 x 100 relay. Her 11 total medals make her the most decorated Olympic athlete in U.S. track and field history.

Felix enjoyed early international success at 100 meters, winning gold at the World Youth Championships when she was 15. She then broke the national high school record in the 200 during her senior year.

WOW FACTOR

9

U.S outdoor titles Felix won in her career, six in the 200 and three in the 400.

Who is the only tennis player to win all four majors and Olympic gold in the same year?

It's known as the Golden Slam, and **Steffi Graf** is the only person who has ever accomplished it. She began the 1988 season with a victory in the Australian Open (against future Hall of Famer Chris Evert), then won the French Open, Wimbledon (against future Hall of Famer Martina Navratilova), the U.S. Open, and the Olympics singles tournament before the year was over.

The native of Germany held the record for most career Grand Slam singles victories in the Open era (22) until Serena Williams broke it in 2017. Graf also topped the world rankings for a record 186 straight weeks, a mark she now shares with Williams.

Some athletes have the power to transcend sports and create seismic shifts in our culture

WONDER
WOMEN

Which hockey superstar competed in both the Summer and Winter Olympics?

Before retiring in 2017, **Hayley Wickenheiser** was considered the greatest female hockey player in the world. She had certainly earned the title. In 1994, the native of Shaunavon, Saskatchewan, led Team Canada to the first of seven IHHF women's world championships, and she won four Olympic hockey gold medals and one silver.

Wickenheiser's athletic prowess wasn't limited to the ice, however. She competed for Canada's softball team at the 2000 Sydney Olympics, becoming one of a handful of Canadian women to compete in both the Winter and Summer Games. Wickenheiser is the all-time Olympic hockey leader in points (51).

DID YOU KNOW?

In 1998 and 1999, Wickenheiser was invited to the Philadelphia Flyers' NHL rookie camp. And when her shot found the back of the net in a February 2003 game for Salamat Kirkkonummen in Finland, Wickenheiser became the first woman to score a goal in men's professional hockey.

Who was the first woman to drive in the Indianapolis 500 and the Daytona 500?

They are the two most prestigious events in American racing, and during a three-month stretch in 1977, **Janet Guthrie** became the first woman to compete in both. First came the Daytona 500, where Guthrie came in 12th and was the race's top rookie. At the Indy 500, Guthrie didn't fare as well, finishing only 27 laps, but in 1978 she was ninth.

Her sixth-place finish at Bristol Motor Speedway in 1977 was the best by a woman in a NASCAR race until Danica Patrick tied it in 2014.

In Guthrie's autobiography, she recounts that life on the track was difficult because so many people did not accept her. And her career effectively ended in 1980 because she could not get sponsors to pay for her car. "If I contributed some small bit to the changing perception of women's abilities, I am glad of that," she wrote. "It was not the reason I did what I did. I drove race cars because I could not do otherwise; because it was an obsession and a passion."

Who was the first woman to play pro baseball?

She played in men's amateur leagues until she was 60 years old, but it was the two seasons she played in the Negro leagues, for the Indianapolis Clowns and the Kansas City Monarchs in the early 1950s, that earned **Toni Stone** a spot in the history books.

The first woman to play professional baseball with men grew up in St. Paul, Minnesota, which recognized her by declaring March 6, 1990, Marcenia Toni Stone Alberga Day. In 1997, one year after she died, a baseball field at a sports complex in St. Paul was dedicated in her honor.

Which swimmer won three gold medals at the Paralympics when she was only 12?

Born without parts of her lower legs, **Jessica Long** was adopted from a Russian orphanage when she was 13 months old. Before she was two, she had both legs amputated below the knee. She began swimming competitively when she was 10 and made a splash at the 2004 Paralympics, winning three gold medals. Two years later, at the 2006 Paralympic world championships, she broke five world records and won nine—nine!—gold medals. The following spring, Long became the first Paralympian to win the Sullivan Award, which is given to the top amateur athlete in the U.S.

Through the 2022 Games, Long has won 29 total medals to become the second-most-decorated U.S. Paralympian in history.

WOW FACTOR

12

Long's age at the 2004 Paralympic Games. She won three gold medals.

FAST FACT:
Spooner gave birth to her son, Rory, in December 2022. Four weeks later she was back training on the ice, and missed only eight weeks of hockey in total.

Who was the first MVP in Professional Women's Hockey League history?

The inaugural season of the Professional Women's Hockey League in 2023 was filled with many firsts, from the first pick in the first draft (Taylor Heise) to the first game (New York vs. Toronto) to the first Walter Cup champion (Minnesota). No one had a better first season than Toronto's **Natalie Spooner**, who was named the league's first Most Valuable Player. Spooner led the league in goals (20) and points (27) and led her team to a top seed before suffering a knee injury. She was also named to the PWHL's First Team All-Stars.

Which tennis player has won the most matches in the Open era?

Over her professional tennis career, **Martina Navratilova** pretty much did it all. She won championships in singles (18 Grand Slams), doubles (31), and mixed doubles (10), the last of these titles coming in mixed doubles at the 2006 U.S. Open, when she was 49. Navratilova won 2,189 matches, more than any tennis player since 1968, when professionals began to compete.

She simply dominated the sport in the 1980s and was named the Associated Press Athlete of the Year in 1983 and 1986. Navratilova, who became a broadcaster after retiring, is also a vocal supporter of LGBT rights.

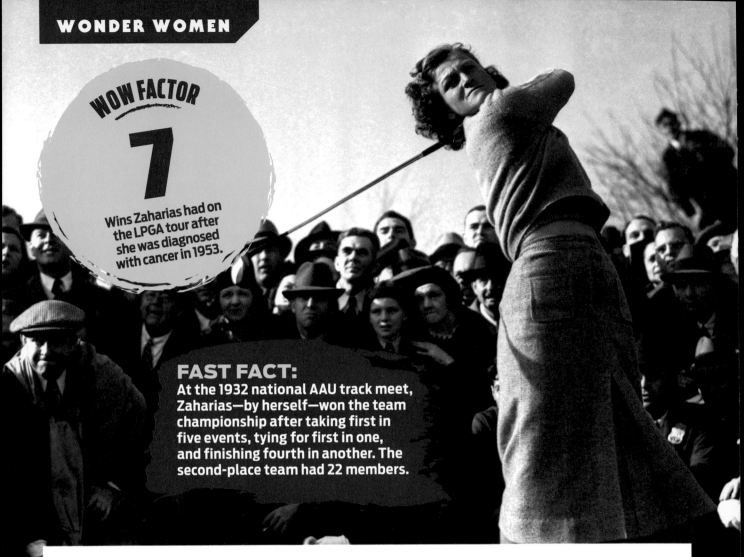

WOW FACTOR

7

Wins Zaharias had on the LPGA tour after she was diagnosed with cancer in 1953.

FAST FACT:
At the 1932 national AAU track meet, Zaharias—by herself—won the team championship after taking first in five events, tying for first in one, and finishing fourth in another. The second-place team had 22 members.

Who was the greatest athlete of the first half of the 20th century?

The world has seen faster and stronger athletes since 1950, but no one in the last 100 years has been as multi-talented as **Babe Didrikson Zaharias**. When she returned home to Texas after taking gold in the javelin and the hurdles, and silver in the high jump at the 1932 Olympics, 10,000 people showed up at the airport to cheer for the 21-year-old phenom.

Zaharias excelled at every sport she tried. She took up golf seriously in her early 20s and won the U.S. and the British amateurs in 1946 and 1947, respectively. She was instrumental in the founding of the LPGA tour in 1950 and won 31 tournaments in six years.

She was a three-time Amateur Athletic Union All-America basketball player and led her team to a national title in 1931. And she was an all-star softball athlete who pitched in MLB exhibition games. To stay in tip-top shape, she used various methods of training, including boxing.

The day that she died of cancer at only 45, President Eisenhower said, "She . . . won the admiration of every person in the United States, all sports people all over the world, and in her gallant fight against cancer, she put up one of the kind of fights that inspire us all."

Who was the oldest woman to score in a World Cup final?

On July 7, 2019, in the 61st minute of the 2019 World Cup final against the Netherlands, **Megan Rapinoe** scored a goal on a penalty kick drawn by teammate Alex Morgan. After scoring, the U.S. women's co-captain posed near the corner flag in celebration: arms outstretched, chin up, and head tipped back. At age 34 and two days, Rapinoe became the oldest goal scorer in a FIFA Women's World Cup final. The U.S. won 2–0 to win their fourth World Cup title.

That goal was the culmination of one of the most accomplished careers in the history of women's soccer. Rapinoe also won gold with the national team at the 2012 London Summer Olympics and the 2015 FIFA Women's World Cup. Her cross to Abby Wambach in the 122nd minute of the 2011 World Cup quarterfinal against Brazil was the latest goal ever scored in a World Cup match.

Rapinoe has also worked as an activist for equality. She received national attention when she kneeled during the national anthem at an international match in 2016 to express solidarity with NFL quarterback Colin Kaepernick. In 2019, she led her teammates to sue the U.S. Soccer Federation for equal pay three months before the World Cup. In recognition of her leadership on and off the pitch, Rapinoe was named SPORTS ILLUSTRATED's 2019 Sportsperson of the Year.

WOW FACTOR

6

Number of goals Rapinoe scored during the 2019 FIFA Women's World Cup as the best player.

Who won world titles in two sports in the same year?

Let's just say that 1976 was a very good year for **Sheila Young-Ochowicz**. At the Olympics in February, the speedskater won gold in the 500 meters, silver in the 1,500, and bronze in the 1,000. Then she won the world sprint speedskating championship. That summer, she took first at the world sprint-cycling championship. Over her career, she snagged three world championships in each sport. "You could say I'm a pretty competitive person," she said after that 1976 cycling title. "I like winning at things."

Who was nicknamed the Queen of Diving?

When she first began diving at the age of eight, **Fu Mingxia** didn't know how to swim. "My instructor had to pull me out of the pool with a piece of rope," she said before the 1996 Olympics. At those Games, Fu added to her collection of two world championships and an Olympic gold, defending her title in the 10-meter platform and also winning gold in the three-meter springboard. In 2000, she took gold in springboard again and silver in the springboard synchronized event, becoming the first female diver to win gold in three straight Olympics.

Who scored the clinching goal in the 2019 Women's World Cup final?

Midfielder **Rose Lavelle** had already represented the United States in a number of tournaments heading into the 2019 Women's World Cup, including at multiple youth levels, and she scored the senior team's winning goal in the 2018 CONCACAF championship game against Canada. Lavelle started six games for the U.S. at the 2019 Cup in France, scoring three goals. Her most memorable may have been the team's second goal in the final against the Netherlands, which essentially put the match out of reach and gave the U.S. its second consecutive World Cup championship. Heading into the 2024 Paris Olympics, Lavelle has played in 100 games as a member of the USWNT.

FAST FACT:
Lavelle was the number one overall pick in the 2017 NWSL draft by the Boston Breakers. She currently plays for the NJ/NY Gotham FC.

Who was the star of the U.S. Olympic volleyball team that won silver in 1984?

Leading up to the 1984 Olympics, SPORTS ILLUSTRATED called Flo Hyman "a phenomenal athlete who seemingly strikes the ball with enough ferocity to rearrange the grain in a wood floor." Wow. Indeed, the 6'5" Hyman, who had missed the Olympics in 1980 when the U.S. boycotted the Games, was one of the most powerful and graceful volleyball players of all time. She anchored the U.S. squad that was expected to win gold in 1984 but settled for silver. It was still the first-ever medal for Team USA.

Hyman was named Best Attacker at the 1981 World Cup and helped the U.S. win bronze at the 1982 world championships. She died when she was only 31, while playing a match in Japan. She had not known that she had been born with a genetic condition that had led to a heart problem.

WOW FACTOR

3

Seasons Hyman earned All-America honors in volleyball at the University of Houston.

Who was the first woman to win Olympic gold in four different events?

She set a world record in the 200-meter dash in 1956 when she was 18 years old, but **Betty Cuthbert** still didn't think she would make the team for that year's Olympics, which were being held in her native Australia. So she bought a ticket to attend the Games as a fan. Not only did Cuthbert make the team, but she also became a national hero and a world-famous track star after winning gold in the 100, the 200, and as part of the 4 × 100 relay team.

Though she left the 1960 Olympics empty-handed, she returned to the Games and won gold in the 400 meters in 1964, the first year the race was held for women.

In the late 1960s, Cuthbert was diagnosed with multiple sclerosis and over the next several decades was an advocate for those with the illness.

Who was the first woman to drive a full NASCAR Cup schedule?

She was already an accomplished open-wheel racer in IndyCar when **Danica Patrick** made her stock car debut in 2010 in one of NASCAR's lower circuits. "I had so much fun in the race car today," she said afterward. "I can't wait to do it again."

Patrick steadily moved up the ranks of the sport, advancing from the ARCA Racing Series to the Nationwide Series, and finally, to the Sprint Cup Series, NASCAR's top tier, in 2012. She ran 10 races that year, and in 2013 she ran 36 out of 36, the first time a woman had raced every event on the schedule.

In seven years of Cup racing, Patrick had seven top 10s but never averaged higher than 20th in points. Like Janet Guthrie before her, Patrick faced criticism from fellow drivers and from those who didn't think she belonged in NASCAR. "It's something that hasn't been uncommon for my entire career," she said in 2013. "It doesn't get to me. The haters are louder than the nice people, unfortunately."

DID YOU KNOW?

From 2005 through 2011, Patrick raced on the IndyCar circuit, and she reached more than a few milestones. She won the 2008 Indy Japan 300 to become the first woman to win an IndyCar race. In her Indianapolis 500 debut, in 2005, she became the first woman to lead a lap at Indy and ended up fourth, the highest finish by a woman in the race. She topped that four years later, when she finished third, then returned in 2018 for her final professional race as a full-time driver.

Which softball player also trained to be an orthopedic surgeon?

FAST FACT:
When she was 13, Richardson became the youngest athlete to play in the Women's Major Fastpitch national championship.

Softball only became an Olympic sport in 1996. By then **Dot Richardson** had helped Team USA win three world championships (1986, 1990, 1994) and four Pan-American Games. The Summer Olympics in Atlanta in 1996 was softball's big close-up, and Richardson and her teammates put on a show.

The three-time All-America at UCLA hit what would be the winning home run against China in that inaugural gold medal game. At the time, she had just finished medical school and was in the middle of a five-year stint at a hospital working in orthopedic surgery. The year after she finished, she helped Team USA win gold at the 2000 Olympics.

Who stole 109 bases in 1946 to lead the All-American Girls Professional Baseball League?

Her local paper called her "a speed demon on the base paths." A former major league player referred to her as the "fanciest-fielding first baseman I've ever seen, man or woman."

In short, **Dorothy Kamenshek** could flat-out play ball. So during World War II, the lefty from Cincinnati joined the hundreds of women who were invited to Chicago's Wrigley Field in 1943 to try out for the AAGPBL's four original teams.

She made the Rockford (Illinois) Peaches and won the league batting title in 1946 and 1947. She also led the Peaches to the championship four times and made the All-Star team in seven of her 10 seasons.

In 1950, the Fort Lauderdale club of the Class B Florida International League, a men's minor league, tried to buy her contract, but the board of directors for the AAGPBL rejected the offer, saying, "Rockford couldn't afford to lose her."

In the 1992 movie *A League of Their Own*, the character Dottie Hinson, portrayed as the star of the AAGPBL, was partially based on Kamenshek.

WOW FACTOR

3

Number of times Devers was a world indoor champion in the 60-meter dash, in 1993, 1997, and 2004.

Atlanta 1996

Which sprinter was a 10-time U.S. 100-meter hurdle champion?

In the 1990s, **Gail Devers** traded U.S. and world records in the 100-meter hurdles with fellow UCLA star Jackie Joyner-Kersee, her training partner under Joyner-Kersee's husband, Bob Kersee, the Bruins' head coach. Devers was a three-time world champion in the event. However, she made her Olympic impact in a different dash, the 100-meter sprint (without hurdles). She won the race in 1992 and defended her title as the fastest woman in the world at the 1996 Games, where she also won gold in the 4 × 100 relay.

At the prestigious Millrose Games in New York City in 2007, a 40-year-old Devers won the 60-meter indoor hurdles, the event in which she had been a world champion in 2003. "People thought I went away," she said after the Millrose Games. "I always knew I could come back."

Who was the first player to dunk in a WNBA game?

Running down the court on a breakaway in a 2002 game against the Miami Sol, **Lisa Leslie** corralled a pass from L.A. Sparks teammate Latasha Byears. Leslie dribbled once; she dribbled twice. She took two steps with the ball and floated to the basket. Then: Slam! She dunked the ball, becoming the first woman to do so in a WNBA game. Later that summer, she led the Sparks to their second title and earned her second Finals MVP award.

Leslie, who was a three-time All-America at USC, led Team USA to four straight Olympic gold medals, beginning in 1996. She briefly retired after her first Games to pursue a career in modeling, but one year afterward, she was back on the court to play in the inaugural season of the WNBA. "I thought it was a summer league," she said upon her retirement—12 years later! A three-time league MVP and eight-time member of the All-WNBA first-team, Leslie was the league's most famous player and a gracious ambassador for the sport. She joined fellow USC Trojan Cheryl Miller in the basketball Hall of Fame in 2015.

Who is the youngest Olympic medalist in Great Britain's history?

To call **Sky Brown** a skateboarding prodigy understates what the 16-year-old has already accomplished. When she was just eight years old, she became the youngest skater to compete in the Vans US Open. Two years later, Brown turned pro, becoming the youngest professional skateboarder in the world. She then represented Great Britain at the delayed 2020 Tokyo Olympics, the first time skateboarding was included in the Games. Brown took home the bronze medal in the women's park skateboarding event; at just 13 years and 28 days, she is Great Britain's youngest medal winner.

FAST FACT: Brown's dad is English, but moved to the United States when he was a teenager. He and Sky's mom, Mieko, met in Japan, which is where their daughter was born. Sky spends half the school year in Japan and the other half in the U.S.

Which U.S. player kicked the game-winning penalty shot to win the 1999 World Cup?

After one period of overtime, the U.S. and China were still tied at zero in the 1999 World Cup final. It was time for penalty kicks. "Do you think you can make it?" an assistant coach on Team USA asked **Brandi Chastain**.

"Yeah, I do," replied Chastain.

Ten minutes later, she did, breaking the 4–4 tie in penalty kicks. She booted the ball with her left foot because she had been struggling when using her right.

"I told myself, Don't look at the goalkeeper," she said later. "It's probably a good thing I didn't think about the kick itself."

One of the best attacking defenders in the world, Chastain was on the squads that won Olympic gold in 1996 and 2004 and silver in 2000. She was also a member of the U.S. team that won the first Women's World Cup in 1991.

DID YOU KNOW?

China had already missed a penalty kick, so the game ended on Chastain's shot. She took off her jersey to celebrate, as many male soccer players had done before her. Because she was a woman, her decision made news. (She was wearing a Nike sports bra; the company was ecstatic.) She was on magazine covers and landed a coveted spot on Wheaties cereal boxes. Her iconic pose became a symbol of empowerment for girls everywhere.

Which LPGA tour golfer has the most single-season wins?

In 1964, SPORTS ILLUSTRATED called her "the best woman golfer of all time," and **Mickey Wright** was only 29 years old. "She is such a long hitter, so accurate, and so dedicated to the game, that many observers are surprised she does not win every tournament she enters."

True, but she sure did win a lot. One year earlier, she had set the record for single-season victories on the LPGA tour (13), and in 1964, she won 11 tournaments, now tied with Annika Sorenstam for the second-best season of all time.

Though she retired when she was 34—Wright did not enjoy being in the spotlight—she is second on the LPGA tour's all-time wins list (82). She is also second in major tournament wins (13) and ended her career with records for lowest round (62) and most birdies in a round (nine).

DID YOU KNOW?

More than 30,000 people showed up at the Astrodome in Houston, Texas, in 1973 to see King play Bobby Riggs in a much-hyped match that became known as the Battle of the Sexes. She won in straight sets, took home $100,000 in prize money, and scored a victory for the women's movement. In 2017, the story of that match became a movie starring Emma Stone as King.

Which female tennis player received the Presidential Medal of Freedom?

It's the highest honor a civilian can receive in the United States, and in 2009, Barack Obama bestowed the Presidential Medal of Freedom on **Billie Jean King** for her accomplishments on and off the tennis court. King won a record 20 championships at Wimbledon (in singles, doubles, and mixed doubles, now tied with Martina Navratilova for most in history) and was the first woman to earn SPORTS ILLUSTRATED Sportsperson of the Year honors (in 1972). King was also a champion of equality as a player, president of the Women's Tennis Association, and founder of the Women's Sports Foundation. In 2006, the tennis complex in Queens, New York, that hosts the U.S. Open was renamed in King's honor.

> **" [Sport] teaches us about daily living. Certain things don't always go our way. Sometimes we have to lose and we all must face it. Ups and downs. Hills and valleys. That's what sport is all about. That's what life is about, too."**
>
> **—in 1972, upon being named SPORTS ILLUSTRATED Sportsperson of the Year alongside UCLA coach John Wooden**

These stars broke down barriers and set sports on a new path

TRAIL

BLAZERS

Who was the first girl to pitch a shutout in the Little League World Series?

The summer before she started eighth grade was a momentous one for **Mo'ne Davis**. After throwing a complete-game, two-hit shutout against an all-boys' team from Tennessee in the 2014 Little League World Series, she became an overnight sensation, receiving messages on social media from First Lady Michelle Obama, NBA superstar Kevin Durant, and many others. She struck out eight and did not walk a single batter in a 4–0 victory for her All-Star team from Philadelphia. "It was nerve-racking, but I kept cool," she said. "My team told me, 'Go out and do what you do and we'll back you up.' They did. But me getting a shutout? I was a little shocked. I did it before, but this was a bigger stage."

The first Little Leaguer to appear on the cover of SPORTS ILLUSTRATED, Davis played softball and graduated with a degree in communications from Hampton University.

DID YOU KNOW?

Mo'ne, the 18th girl to play in the LLWS, was on the cover of the August 25, 2014, edition of SPORTS ILLUSTRATED and also graced the front of the December issue of SI KIDS, having been named the SportsKid of the Year. "I just thought I was going to play baseball in the summer, have fun with my friends, then go back to school this fall," she told SI during the LLWS. "But now, because everything got so big and because we're doing well, I do feel like a role model."

WOW FACTOR

14

Batters Davis struck out in two starts in the 2014 LLWS. She only allowed one walk in 8⅓ innings.

Who is the first Asian woman to win the individual all-around gold medal at the Olympics?

At the 2020 Tokyo Olympics, gymnast **Suni Lee** admitted she thought she was competing for second place. But when teammate and all-around favorite Simone Biles withdrew, Lee seized the moment and replaced her on floor exercise in the team final. Her performance helped the U.S. win the silver medal. Lee then took the individual all-around, becoming the fifth consecutive American and the first Hmong American to win the gold medal. "My community is so amazing," said Lee. "They were all watching together and got to see me win a gold medal. Many people from the Hmong community don't reach their goals, and I want them to know you can reach your dreams and don't ever give up. You never know."

Who was the first female athlete to play in the NHL?

During a Tampa Bay Lightning preseason game in 1992, 20-year-old **Manon Rheaume** became the first woman to play in an NHL game, stopping seven of the nine shots that came her way. She only appeared in one other exhibition, but she went on to play five seasons in the minors. "At the time I didn't realize what I was doing," she said a decade later. "I look at the game, how fast it is, how hard the guys shoot, and I can't believe I was there." The native of Quebec won world championships with Canada's women's team in 1992 and 1994, and helped the squad take silver at the 1998 Olympics.

FAST FACT:
When she was 19, Rheaume became the first woman to play in the Quebec Major Junior Hockey League.

FAST FACT:
Clark, who has won more than 70 events in her career, had a breakout moment when she won the U.S. Snowboard Grand Prix title as a 17-year-old.

WOW FACTOR

3

Medals Clark won in her first four Olympics—one gold and two bronze—more than any snowboarder at the time.

Which snowboarder has more halfpipe medals than any woman in X Games history?

She has 14 X Games medals, seven of them gold, but **Kelly Clark** has done more than win hardware during her celebrated snowboarding career. She has changed the way athletes compete. She was the first woman to land a 1080—a move that requires three full rotations in midair—in halfpipe competition.

Clark, who attended Mount Snow Academy while growing up in Vermont, was racing on skis as a first-grader. By the time she was 11, however, she had made her preference known: She would much rather be snowboarding than skiing.

She was 19 when she won her first Olympic medal, a gold in 2002, just four years after the sport made its debut at the Games.

Who has the longest winning streak in tennis history?

Is it Serena Williams? No. Roger Federer? Wrong. Rafa? Nope. Pete Sampras, or Monica Seles, or Steffi Graf, or Novak Djokovic? All no. The holder of the longest winning streak in tennis history is **Esther Vergeer**. The Dutch athlete won 470 consecutive wheelchair tennis matches.

The size of the court, net height, and rackets are the same in wheelchair tennis, but the ball can bounce twice before being returned. No one has dominated the game like Vergeer: over the course of her career, Vergeer won 700 singles matches and lost just 25. She went undefeated in singles for 10 straight years. She won 43 major titles and seven Paralympic gold medals, and was the world top-ranked player from 1999 to her retirement in February 2013. During the streak Vergeer lost only 18 sets and was taken to match point only once.

Who was the first woman to play in a men's pro basketball league?

Known for her physical style on the court, point guard **Nancy Lieberman** was the preeminent player of her day. She became the youngest basketball player to ever win an Olympic medal when she helped Team USA earn silver in 1976 as a 17-year-old. She then led Old Dominion to consecutive national titles (1979, 1980) and a 72–2 record as a junior and senior.

Her career was far from over after her run of dominance at ODU. She played in the New York Pro Summer League alongside men after graduation to stay in shape, then played for the Dallas Diamonds in two different women's pro leagues. In 1986, the men's United States Basketball League called, and Lieberman played for the Springfield Fame that year and the Long Island Knights in 1987. She went on to become a head coach in the WNBA with the Detroit Shock and an assistant in the NBA with the Sacramento Kings.

Said Lieberman upon being inducted into the Hall of Fame in 1996, "Basketball has given me . . . my confidence, my self-esteem, the ability to share with teammates, to be responsible, to learn how to win, and also to learn how to lose."

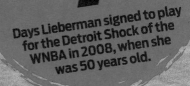

WOW FACTOR

7

Days Lieberman signed to play for the Detroit Shock of the WNBA in 2008, when she was 50 years old.

FAST FACT:
Rudolph was one of the famed Tennessee State Tigerbelles who combined to win 13 Olympic gold medals under coach Ed Temple.

Which sprinter overcame paralysis to win three Olympic gold medals?

When she was four years old, **Wilma Rudolph**, the 20th of 22 children growing up in a poor household in Tennessee, had double pneumonia and scarlet fever at the same time. She was so sick that she almost died, and her left leg was paralyzed. It wasn't until she was eight years old that she began to walk, using a leg brace. Three years later she was able to play basketball, and by the time she was 16, she was on the U.S. Olympic track and field team. She helped the 4 × 100-meter relay team win bronze at the 1956 Games.

When she returned to the Olympics in 1960, she became a superstar. She won the 100, the 200, and anchored the winning 4 × 100 relay team to gold. "I just run," she said afterward. "I don't know why I run so fast."

Who is the first woman to win the main event at WrestleMania?

When Charlotte Flair, Ronda Rousey, and **Becky Lynch** met in the main event of WrestleMania 35 at MetLife Stadium in 2019, it represented a milestone; never before had women been featured in the final match at WWE's signature event. While Flair came from a family steeped in professional wrestling and Rousey brought her MMA fame with her, it was Lynch who was the fan favorite and ultimately won the match and both the Raw and SmackDown Women's championships. In the years since, Lynch, known at times as "Big Time Becks" and "The Man," has become one of the biggest stars in her industry.

DID YOU KNOW?

Lynch, whose real name is Rebecca Quin, published her autobiography, *The Man: Not Your Average Average Girl*, in 2024. It was an instant *New York Times* bestseller.

WOW FACTOR

27

Minutes (plus 14 seconds) by which Switzer won the women's division of the 1974 New York City Marathon, the largest margin of victory in the race's history.

Who was the first woman to officially complete the Boston Marathon?

No woman had ever entered the Boston Marathon, so three weeks before the 1967 race, 20-year-old Syracuse University student **Kathrine Switzer** completed 31 miles on a training run, just to be sure she was ready to tackle the 26.2-mile race. The next day, she signed up for Boston as K.V. Switzer.

On a snowy Patriots' Day, April 19, Switzer, her boyfriend, and her coach lined up at the start, and they were off! Four miles into the race, an official spotted her. "Get out of my race and give me those numbers," he shouted as he tried to rip off her race bib. She got away from him and ran all 26.2 miles despite blisters popping on the arches of her feet. She went on to run the race eight more times, including in 2017 to commemorate the 50th anniversary of her accomplishment.

WOW FACTOR

.259

The point total by which Douglas beat silver-medalist Viktoria Komova of Russia in the 2012 Olympics individual all-around event.

Who was the first American gymnast to win an individual and a team gold medal at the same Olympic Games?

For gymnast **Gabby Douglas**, sacrifice paid off. Big time. At the 2012 London Olympics, Douglas, at age 16, became the first U.S. gymnast to win an individual and a team gold medal at the same Games. Douglas won the individual all-around, in which each athlete competes in four disciplines—the vault, uneven bars, balance beam, and floor. She also won gold in the team competition, along with her Fierce Five teammates, Aly Raisman, McKayla Maroney, Kyla Ross, and Jordyn Wieber.

Douglas's road to Olympic gold was not an easy one, though. She moved away from her family in Virginia Beach, Virginia, at the age of 14 to train with legendary coach Liang Chow in West Des Moines, Iowa. Originally her mom said no way to Douglas leaving home (and moving halfway across the country), but her older sisters convinced their mother otherwise. Douglas missed her family, but she never gave up her dream.

FAST FACT:
Douglas was injured during training for the 2024 Summer Olympics in Paris. She intends to try to make the team again in 2028.

WOW FACTOR

171

Golf tournaments Gibson played on the LPGA tour from 1963 through 1977.

Who was the first Black tennis player to compete in the U.S. National Championships?

When she won the 1957 U.S. Open, **Althea Gibson** received the trophy from Vice President Richard Nixon. "I hope to wear my crown with dignity and humility," she said. Gibson indeed displayed great dignity and humility throughout a brief but phenomenal tennis career during which she won 56 tournaments, five singles Grand Slams, and five doubles Grand Slams in eight years.

In 1950, she had become the first Black woman to play in the U.S. National Championships, which was later renamed the U.S. Open. She didn't win her first major, the French Championships (now the French Open), until 1956. The following year she won the Australian Championships (now the Australian Open) in doubles competition, and in singles at Wimbledon and the U.S. Open. She won the latter two tournaments again in 1958. Before her 1957 U.S. Open victory, she appeared on the cover of SPORTS ILLUSTRATED. "Her forceful game has reached the point," the story said, "where she seems to win almost without trying."

Gibson was far from finished with professional sports when her tennis career ended: She went on to become the first Black golfer to join the LPGA tour.

Who was the first WNBA player to score at least 25 points in eight straight games?

Las Vegas Aces star **A'ja Wilson** was a hometown star made very, very good. A native of South Carolina, she stayed in-state to lead the University of South Carolina to the 2017 national championship. After the Aces made her the first pick in the 2018 draft, she won the Rookie of the Year award and then earned her first WNBA MVP award in 2020. She won her second MVP award in 2022, and in that year and 2023 was named the Finals MVP as Las Vegas won back-to-back championships. Wilson continued her tear to start the 2024 season, scoring between 28 and 36 points in eight consecutive games, a new WNBA record.

Who was the first woman to reach the summit of Mount Everest?

In May 1975, 35-year-old Japanese mountaineer **Junko Tabei** led 14 women on an ascent of the 29,029-foot peak. Two-thirds of the way up Everest, while the group slept, an avalanche buried the climbers. They survived thanks to the six Sherpas, or guides, on their expedition, who pulled them out of the snow. Tabei was unable to walk at first but was determined to continue. She resumed the ascent two days later and became the first woman, and 36th person, to summit the world's tallest mountain.

In addition to becoming the first woman to climb the highest peaks on each continent, a feat she accomplished in 1992, Tabei was an environmentalist and preservationist. She opened the door for female climbers everywhere but especially in Japan, where women were discouraged from being adventurous.

She earned fame but shied away from the perks that came with it. "Climbing the mountain," she said, "is its own reward."

Who was the first woman to compete in seven swimming events at one Olympics?

At the 2012 London Games, 17-year-old **Missy Franklin** became the first woman to swim in seven events at one Olympics. She won the 100-meter and 200-meter backstroke, the 4 x 200-meter freestyle relay, and the 4 x 100-meter medley relay. Nicknamed Missy the Missile, she started swimming at the age of five; her dad calls her now-size 13 feet "built-in flippers." After winning five medals in London, Franklin returned home and continued to swim for her high school. She then went on to compete at the University of California. She won another gold at the 2016 Games in Rio de Janeiro.

Which siblings were each selected first overall in the WNBA draft?

Sisters **Nneka** and **Chiney Ogwumike** aren't twins, though their accomplishments on the basketball court have been nearly identical. They both played at Cypress-Fairbanks High School in Texas, where they each were named the Gatorade girls' basketball national player of the year (Nneka in 2008, Chiney in 2010). They both played for Stanford, where they were named Pac-12 Player of the Year twice (Nneka in 2010 and '12, Chiney in 2013 and '14). They both were selected first overall in the WNBA draft—Nneka by the Los Angeles Sparks in 2012; Chiney by the Connecticut Sun in 2014. Nneka was the Finals MVP with the Sparks in 2016 and is an eight-time All-Star entering 2024; Chiney announced her retirement in 2023 and is currently a basketball analyst for ESPN.

Who was the first NCAA coach to reach 1,000 victories?

When **Pat Summitt** arrived at the University of Tennessee to coach basketball in 1974, she drove the team van. Women's basketball finally became an NCAA championship sport in 1981–82, and Summitt's Lady Vols were considered the elite program for two decades, winning eight national championships between 1987 and 2008 and appearing in five other title games.

The court at the basketball arena was named the Summitt in 2005. One year later, she became the first women's basketball coach to earn $1 million a year. Summitt retired in 2012 with more wins (1,098) than anyone in women's or men's college basketball history. She suffered from Alzheimer's and in the last years of her life worked to raise awareness about the disease.

WOW FACTOR

18

Number of times Summitt's Vols reached the Final Four of the NCAA women's basketball tournament.

DID YOU KNOW?

Pat Head (Summitt was her married name) played basketball at Tennessee-Martin and on the U.S. Olympic team that won silver at the 1976 Games (two years after she took the Tennessee job). She went on to coach Team USA to gold at the 1984 Olympics.

WOW FACTOR

97.4

The percentage of free throws that Delle Donne made in 2019, making 114 of her 117 attempts from the line.

Who was the first player in WNBA history to record a 50-40-90 shooting season?

One of the WNBA's stars, **Elena Delle Donne**, at one point quit playing basketball. One of the most coveted recruits in the country as a senior in high school, Delle Donne committed to play for the University of Connecticut. But just two days after arriving in Storrs in the summer of 2008, Delle Donne returned home. She enrolled at the University of Delaware and played volleyball as a freshman; but not basketball.

During the spring of her freshman year, she decided to give basketball another chance. She joined the Blue Hens for the 2009–10 season and averaged 26.7 points per game as a redshirt freshman. As a junior, she led the nation in scoring with an average of 28.1 points per game. Following her college career, Delle Donne was selected second overall in the 2013 WNBA Draft by the Chicago Sky. Delle Donne played for the Sky for five seasons before she was traded to the Washington Mystics in 2017.

Delle Donne led the Mystics to the WNBA Finals in 2019. That season, she became the first player in WNBA history to shoot at least 50 percent from the field, 40 percent from three-point range, and 90 percent from the free throw line for a season. Only eight NBA players have accomplished this feat: Larry Bird, Steve Nash, Mark Price, Reggie Miller, Dirk Nowitzki, Kevin Durant, Stephen Curry, and Malcolm Brogdon.

Who is the youngest player ever to qualify for the main draw at Wimbledon?

When the Wimbledon Championships began in 2019, American phenom **Coco Gauff** was only a few months past her 15th birthday. Nevertheless, after winning four matches during a qualifying tournament prior to the event, Gauff made history by becoming the youngest qualifier to reach the main draw in the Open era. Her run didn't stop there: she upset five-time champion Venus Williams in her opening match, then advanced to the fourth round before losing to eventual Wimbledon winner Simona Halep. Gauff later won the U.S. Open, in 2023, and has been ranked as high as number three in the world.

DID YOU KNOW?

Gauff grew up idolizing Serena and Venus Williams, and made that clear to Venus after defeating her at Wimbledon in 2019. "I was just telling her thank you for everything she's done for the sport," Gauff said. "She's been an inspiration for many people. I was just really telling her thank you."

Who was the first woman to win Triple Crown and Breeders' Cup races?

Growing up in Michigan, **Julie Krone** learned to ride before she learned to walk. She got her start as a groom and an exercise rider at famed Churchill Downs in Kentucky before she was 16. At 17, she won her first race, at Tampa Bay Downs in 1980. Through the early days of her career, she encountered many obstacles: trainers and owners who didn't want to hire her, fellow jockeys who didn't want to ride with her, and plenty of fans who didn't think women should be jockeys.

But she was good, and before she had turned 25, she had 1,200 wins. She was the first woman to win a riding title at a major track (in 1987 at New Jersey racecourses Monmouth Park, the Meadowlands, and Atlantic City); the first to win a Triple Crown race (the 1993 Belmont Stakes astride Colonial Affair); and the first to win a Breeders' Cup race (in 2003 aboard Halfbridled). In 2000, Krone became the first woman inducted into the National Museum of Racing's Hall of Fame.

WOW FACTOR

3,704

Victories Krone had when she retired in 2004. She was the first woman to surpass 3,500 wins.

Who was the first woman to swim the English Channel?

The final three hours of her 14-hour, 31-minute swim from Cape Gris-Nez, France, across the English Channel were brutal for **Gertrude Ederle**. The current pushed against her, and rain pounded the choppy water that August day in 1926 as she tried to become the first woman to complete the 20.9-mile swim. She had been disqualified during her attempt in 1925, after one of her support-team members touched her. (Her team thought she was drowning; she was just resting.)

In 1926, she fought against the current until it turned in her favor, and when she waded ashore in Kingsdown, England, Ederle had finished the swim two hours faster than any of the five men before her. She returned to the States, where an estimated two million people showed up in New York City for a ticker-tape parade in her honor.

These women set new standards for excellence

RECORD BREAKERS

Who has scored more goals than anyone in U.S. national soccer team history?

No soccer player has been better at heading the ball into the net than **Abby Wambach**, so it was not surprising that one of the four goals she scored for the U.S. women's national team in a 5–0 win over South Korea in 2013 was a header. Oh, and that header, her 159th goal, made Wambach the national team's all-time leading scorer among women and men.

"It's just a mathematical equation," the 5'11" Wambach said of how she became so successful at knocking the ball with her noggin. "I'm taller. I can jump. And when you're shooting with your head, it's impossible for goalkeepers to know where the ball is going." She retired in 2015 with 184 goals, two Olympic gold medals, and a record six U.S. Soccer Female Athlete of the Year awards.

She capped off her career by helping Team USA win the World Cup, the major honor that had eluded her.

FAST FACT:
Wambach, the 2012 FIFA Player of the Year, is one of only four Americans to have earned the award. The other three are Mia Hamm (2001, 2002), Carli Lloyd (2015, 2016), and Megan Rapinoe (2019).

> **"** *I'm really proud of the player I was, and I will be proud of the athletes who break my records."*
>
> —in 2017, at the College at Brockport

Who owns the WNBA career scoring record?

In 2017, when she became the leading scorer in WNBA history (7,489 points), **Diana Taurasi** merely gave basketball fans another reason to consider her one of the greatest players of all time.

It would have been devastating for the game (though much better for her opponents) if Taurasi had stuck with her plan to quit the game in favor of soccer when she was 11. Her hiatus from the hard court only lasted for a year, though.

At 18, the nation's top recruit began her career at Connecticut, then led the Huskies to three straight NCAA titles. Shortly after graduation, she helped Team USA win Olympic gold. Taurasi was just getting warmed up: She went on to win four more gold medals, three WNBA titles with the Phoenix Mercury, and five WNBA scoring titles.

WOW FACTOR

6

EuroLeague championships Taurasi has won while playing overseas in the WNBA offseason, a record.

Who is the only female diver to have won back-to-back Olympic golds in springboard and platform?

She was the kind of kid who would do a cannonball off a bridge near her home in California just as a boat was passing underneath to try to splash the passengers. The idea of swimming laps bored **Pat McCormick**, also known as Patsy Pest. But diving? That was fun. Her combination of coordination and timing, along with her eagerness to compete, gave her an instant edge. She began training with the Los Angeles Athletic Club at 16 and only missed the 1948 Olympic team as an 18-year-old by .01 of a point.

McCormick stuck with the sport, sweeping the five U.S. titles in 1951 and going on to win gold in the three-meter springboard and the 10-meter platform at the 1952 Olympics. Her hometown of Long Beach welcomed her home with a parade!

In 1956, less than a year after giving birth to her son, Tim, she was favored to repeat as double champion at that year's Summer Games. After all, she had won 27 national titles by that point. She didn't disappoint, once again taking home two golds and earning Associated Press Female Athlete of the Year.

Who is the only American woman to win six medals in one Olympics?

When she was 10 months old, **Natalie Coughlin** got her start in a pool in her backyard in California. At six, she was competing, and by 16, she had set multiple national age-group records. Slowed by a shoulder injury that year, she narrowly missed the 2000 Olympics. "It was frustrating and depressing," she said, "especially because my earlier times would have made the team." How did Coughlin react? At the 2004 Games, she went out and won five medals: gold in the 100-meter backstroke and with the 4 × 200-meter freestyle relay team; two relay silvers; and bronze in the 100-meter free. She outdid herself in 2008, winning six medals—including a repeat gold in the 100 backstroke—to set the record.

Who is the only runner to simultaneously hold U.S. records at every distance from 800 to 10,000 meters?

In 1974, a pigtailed 15-year-old named **Mary Decker** set world indoor records at 800 meters, and at 880 and 1,000 yards. In 1983, when she was named SPORTS ILLUSTRATED's Sportswoman of the Year, she won the 1,500 and 3,000 meters at the world championships, held seven U.S. records, and had set seven world records in the previous two years. She famously fell in the 3,000 final at the 1984 Olympics but set two world records the following year.

FAST FACT:
To honor the star who grew up about 30 miles west of Chicago in Naperville. Chicago declared September 16, 2021, as "Candace Parker Day."

Who helped lead Chicago to its first WNBA championship?

When the Chicago Sky finished the pandemic-shortened 2021 WNBA season, they carried an unremarkable record of 16–16. But with the help of Chicago-area native **Candace Parker**, the Sky shocked the basketball world, going on a historic playoff run and claiming the championship. A two-time WNBA MVP and Defensive Player of the Year with the Los Angeles Sparks, Parker had signed as a free agent with the Sky after 13 seasons in L.A. She averaged 13.3 points and a team-high 8.4 rebounds per game during the regular season, then put her championship experience to work in the playoffs, as the Sky won two single-elimination games, followed by an upset of the top-seeded Connecticut Sun in the semifinals before beating the Phoenix Mercury in the finals. Parker won a third title, this time with the Las Vegas Aces in 2023, before announcing her retirement in 2024. It capped an incredible career for Parker, who won two national player of the year awards for back-to-back champions at the University of Tennessee, and then became the first player to be named the WNBA's Rookie of the Year and MVP in the same season.

Which swimmer holds the record for most world championships?

When **Katie Ledecky** won the 1,500 meters at the 2017 world championships by 19 seconds (yes, you read that correctly), she brought her career gold medal total at the event to 12, a record for female swimmers. By the end of the competition, she had 14. She has simply dominated freestyle events, winning in the 200-, 400-, 800-, and 1,500-meter races, and in both relays. In 2023 she became the first swimmer to win six golds in the same event at the world championships. It was also her 16th individual world title, the most of any swimmer in history.

Ledecky was only 15 and the youngest member of Team USA when she won the 800 at the 2012 Olympics. At the 2016 Games, where she was again the youngest U.S. swimmer, she became the first athlete to sweep the 200, 400, and 800 meters in nearly 50 years, and she earned gold and silver in two relays. At the 2020 Tokyo Olympics, Ledecky won two gold medals and two silvers, making her the most decorated U.S. female athlete for the second straight Summer Games. She qualified for the 2024 Olympic team with a first-place finish in the 400-meter freestyle.

DID YOU KNOW?

By the time the 2016 Olympics were over, Ledecky was considered one of the greatest swimmers of all time. She set a world record in the 400 freestyle and lowered her own world record in the 800 by nearly two seconds. In the latter race, her last of the Games, she won by 11 seconds.

FAST FACT:
At Stanford, Ledecky became the second freshman to ever win the Honda Cup Award, given to the nation's most outstanding female collegiate athlete.

Who is the youngest woman to win an Olympic snowboarding gold medal?

Competing at her first Olympics, the 2018 Pyeongchang Games, **Chloe Kim** became the youngest woman to win an Olympic snowboarding gold medal at 17 years and 296 days. The previous record holder, Kelly Clark, was 19 when she won gold at Salt Lake City 2002. Kim's score of 93.75 on her first run secured her win, as none of the women in the field could top it through two remaining runs. With her gold medal already assured, Kim attempted and landed back-to-back 1080s (three full rotations) on her final run, becoming the first woman to do so at the Olympics.

Who has more World Cup wins than any alpine skier in history?

When it comes to downhill skiing, no one can match the accomplishments of **Mikaela Shiffrin**. When she was 18 years old, she became the youngest slalom gold medalist in Olympic history. (She won a second gold and a silver medal at the 2018 Olympics.) Shiffrin has continued to dominate the slopes, winning five overall World Cup titles and 97 Cup races, the most of any skier in history. Not even a serious knee injury suffered in Italy in 2023 could slow her down; six weeks later, she bested her closest competitor by a whopping 1.24 seconds during an event in Sweden.

WOW FACTOR

414

Shots Stewart blocked while at UConn, a program career record.

Who was the first athlete to win four Final Four Most Outstanding Player awards?

Already recognized as the nation's top player entering her freshman year at the University of Connecticut in 2012, **Breanna Stewart** was expected to do great things during her college career. No one could have anticipated just how great those things would be—except possibly Stewart herself.

After leading the Huskies to four straight NCAA titles and becoming the only women's or men's player to earn four Final Four MOP awards, she said, "I had the perfect ending to a college career. My goal coming in as a freshman at UConn was to win four national championships." Mission accomplished!

Now playing for the WNBA's New York Liberty, Stewart has only continued her winning ways. She is a two-time WNBA MVP and led the Seattle Storm to two championships in 2018 and 2020, and was named the Finals MVP both times. As a member of the U.S. women's national team, Stewart won gold medals at the 2016 and 2020 Olympics and at the 2014 and 2018 FIBA World Cup.

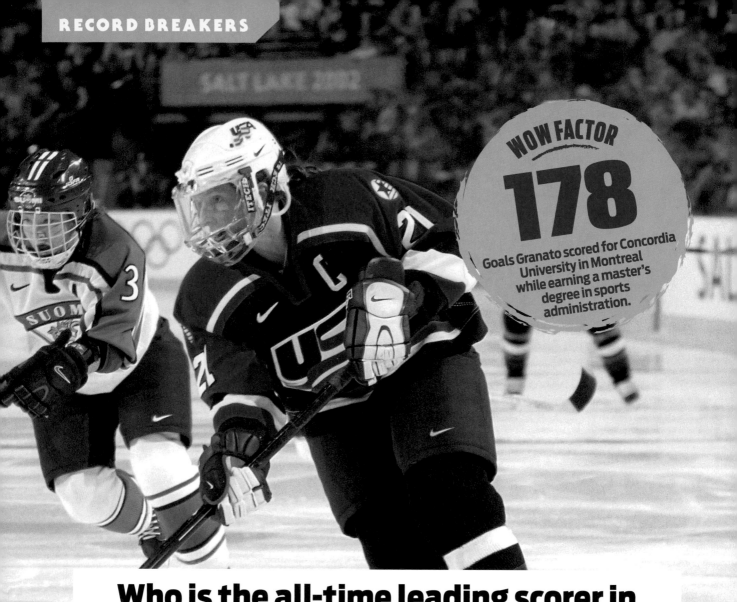

WOW FACTOR

178

Goals Granato scored for Concordia University in Montreal while earning a master's degree in sports administration.

Who is the all-time leading scorer in women's international hockey?

Growing up in a hockey-crazed family in Illinois, **Cammi Granato** played for a boys' team until she was 16, around the time her older brother Tony began his 13-year NHL career. She became a superstar for Providence College and was a founding member of the U.S. women's national team, which took silver at the first-ever women's world championships, in 1990.

Eight years later, at the first Olympics in which women's hockey was included as a sport, Granato was the captain of the U.S. team that upset Canada to win gold.

She was instrumental in helping women's hockey find its footing in the U.S. Granato retired in 2005 with a record 54 international goals. In 2010 she was the first woman inducted into the Hockey Hall of Fame.

Which softball pitcher holds the record for most perfect games in NCAA Division I history?

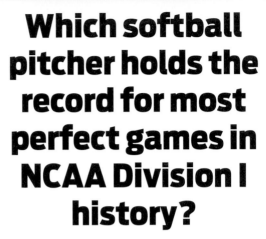

Reporters called her "the most spellbinding pitcher in college softball" and "the best curveball pitcher in the world." In her four seasons at the University of Texas, **Cat Osterman** threw a record nine perfect games and was named national player of the year three times. While with the Longhorns, Osterman helped Team USA win gold at the 2004 Olympics. The lefty also led the squad to silver at the 2008 Games.

Osterman went on to play eight seasons in the National Pro Fastpitch league, earning three pitcher of the year awards, six All-NPF nods, and four championships.

FAST FACT:
In her nine years playing for USA Softball, Osterman was 59–4 with a stunning 0.38 earned run average.

FAST FACT:
Evert worked as a tennis analyst for NBC for 10 years and has been a broadcaster for ESPN since 2011.

WOW FACTOR

125

Consecutive matches Evert won on clay courts, a record among women and men for any surface.

In December 1976, after winning 44 of the 62 tournaments she had entered over a three-year period, Evert was named SPORTS ILLUSTRATED's Sportsperson of the Year. "What makes her a champion who each year moves further and further beyond the reach of mortal tennis players, is grit," the story read. "Chris Evert has true grit. Character. Mental tenacity. She is a clear thinker in a thoughtful game. And she never gives up."

Which tennis player had the longest streak of consecutive years with a Grand Slam victory?

Serena Williams has claimed most of the major women's tennis records, but **Chris Evert** was the darling of American tennis two decades before her, dominating the WTA Tour and winning at least one Grand Slam tournament in each season from 1974 through 1986. During those 13 years, she racked up victories at the Australian Open (two), the French Open (seven), Wimbledon (three), and the U.S. Open (six).

Evert was the first woman to hit the $1 million mark in earnings on the court and was named the Associated Press Female Athlete of the Year four times. She had an intense rivalry with Martina Navratilova, whom Evert faced in 14 Grand Slam finals, winning four.

Who has the most pro golf victories?

During each year that passed in the 1960s and 1970s, **Kathy Whitworth** just kept winning. Eight victories here (1963), another eight there (1965). Nine more in 1966, eight in 1967, and a whopping 10 in 1968!

Then in July 1984, in a sudden-death playoff against Rosie Jones at the Rochester International golf tournament in New York, Whitworth bagged her 85th victory to become the winningest professional golfer in history. Sam Snead, the PGA Tour icon, had previously held the record. "Sam was just great about it," Whitworth, who retired with 88 wins, said years later. "He called me in the press room when it finally happened."

Tiger Woods, who currently has 82 wins on the PGA Tour, is the only active golfer within 45 victories of Whitworth's record.

FAST FACT:
Twice named the Associated Press Female Athlete of the Year, Whitworth won the Vare Trophy, given to the LPGA tour member with the lowest scoring average, a record seven times.

Which sprinter's world records in the 100 and 200 meters have stood since the 1980s?

Known as Flo-Jo, **Florence Griffith Joyner** had flair—she sported colorful, long nails and often one-legged unitards—and was she fast. In fact, she became the fastest woman on the planet when she set a world record to win the 100-meter race at the 1988 U.S. Olympic Trials in Indianapolis (10.49). At the Games that summer, she won gold in the 100 and the 200, setting a world record in the latter (21.34). Both of those marks were still intact at the end of 2023. Her fashion sense brought her notoriety after her retirement in 1988: She was asked to design new uniforms for the NBA's Indiana Pacers. The team sported those duds for seven seasons in the 1990s. Joyner, who was married to track star Jackie Joyner-Kersee's brother, died at 38 after an epileptic seizure.

Who is the most decorated Winter Olympian of all time?

At the 2018 Games, cross-country skier **Marit Bjørgen** of Norway won her 11th, 12th, 13th, and 14th Olympic medals to put her at the top of the list. She then won the 30-kilometer mass start to end the Games with 15 career medals, eight of them gold (tied for most by any Winter Olympian). That haul is pretty impressive on its own, but she has 26 world championship medals as well. She also had 114 World Cup wins, more than twice as many as any other woman.

Bjørgen has excelled at a variety of distances, having competed in the 10K (6.2 miles), 15K, and 30K. She earned her first medal as a 21-year-old at the 2002 Olympics, when Norway's 4 × 5K relay team took silver.

Who is the only swimmer to set American records in all four strokes?

As a 15-year-old with braces on her teeth, **Tracy Caulkins** broke five U.S. records at the 1978 AAU National Short Course Championships. Then she won five golds at the world championships that year. She was gearing up for the 1980 Olympics, but the U.S. boycotted the Games for political reasons. "I suppose I could be over the hill in 1984," she said that summer.

Far from it. When the U.S. Olympic Trials rolled around, the 21-year-old was a 48-time national champ. She made the team, then won the 200- and 400-meter individual medleys and took gold with the U.S. 4 × 100 medley relay team.

Which woman has the most Olympic medals in history?

Growing up in Ukraine, **Larisa Latynina** began ballet lessons when she was 11. One year later, the studio closed, so she took up gymnastics. The woman who entered the sport by chance now has more Olympic medals (18) than anyone except U.S. swimmer Michael Phelps (28).

Competing for the Soviet Union during the 1956, 1960, and 1964 Games, Latynina led her squad to three straight team victories. She also won back-to-back golds in the all-around competition before coming in second to Vera Cáslavská in 1964. (Cáslavská is the only other woman to successfully defend her Olympic all-around title.)

WOW FACTOR

55,646

Number of fans at one of Clark's final preseason games at Iowa, a women's basketball attendance record.

Who is the all-time leading scorer in NCAA Division I basketball history?

In her final regular-season game at the University of Iowa, **Caitlin Clark** scored 35 points and passed LSU's Pete Maravich as college basketball's all-time leading scorer. But setting records was nothing new for Clark, nor does it capture her impact on the sporting world. A two-time national player of the year, Clark's ability to shoot from anywhere on the floor helped change the sport and made her a must-see attraction. She has become a cultural phenomenon, raising the profile of women's basketball and breaking attendance and viewership records everywhere she played; Clark's final three games of the 2024 NCAA tournament each broke the women's college basketball viewership record, including the 18.9 million viewers who tuned in for the national championship game. It was the first time the women's tournament final outdrew the men's. Clark was selected No. 1 overall in the 2024 WNBA draft by the Indiana Fever.

These winners
showed heart
and got results

CHAM

PIONS

Who won four WNBA titles in her first seven seasons in the league?

When she was a freshman at UConn, forward **Maya Moore** was the top scorer for the Huskies and came in second in the Associated Press Player of the Year voting. After four years on campus, she had led the program to a 150–4 record and won two national championships (2009, 2010).

The Minnesota Lynx selected Moore with the first pick in the 2011 WNBA draft—and she just kept on winning. She earned Rookie of the Year while helping the Lynx to the championship that season, then led the team to titles in 2013, 2015, and 2017. And the honors have just kept rolling in: Moore was Finals MVP (2013), league MVP (2014), and was first-team All-WNBA from 2013 through 2017.

WOW FACTOR

149

Games Moore scored in double figures at UConn (out of 154 games played), an NCAA record.

> " *I love all my championships. I love to compete, and when you have the talent, the discipline, the work ethic, and teammates who do the same thing, winning follows you around.*"

—in 2013, to SPORTS ILLUSTRATED

WOW FACTOR

10

Individual golds Thompson won at world championship meets.

Who won more Olympic golds than any female swimmer in history?

Swimming is often thought of as an individual endeavor, but for American **Jenny Thompson**, the sport was very much about teamwork. Over four Olympics, she won a record eight gold medals, all in relays (three in the 4 × 100-meter freestyle, two in the 4 × 200, and three in the 4 × 100 medley). She also won two relay silvers, and silver and bronze in the 100 free in 1992 and 2000, respectively, bringing her total to 12 medals (tied with Americans Dara Torres and Natalie Coughlin for most by a female swimmer).

That's not to say that Thompson didn't have success on her own: In 1992, she became the first U.S. woman in 61 years to break the world record in the 100 free. And in 2004, she won the 50-meter butterfly at the world championships, then retired from swimming so she could complete her final two years at Columbia medical school.

Who was the first athlete to win four world marathon majors in a year?

When she crossed the finish line at the 2013 New York City Marathon, **Tatyana McFadden** became the first person to win four world marathon majors in one year, having also finished first in Boston, London, and Chicago. Through 2023, she had 24 major marathon victories, the most of any female wheelchair racer, and 20 Paralympic medals (eight gold, eight silver, and four bronze), including silver from the 2014 Winter Paralympics in crosscountry skiing.

Born with a condition called spina bifida, McFadden is paralyzed from the waist down. She was adopted from a Russian orphanage when she was six and moved to the U.S. Thanks to lawsuits she filed while in high school in Maryland, students with disabilities must be included in that state's school athletic activities and be allowed to compete against able-bodied athletes.

> " *It's taken a lot of hard work and dedication, trying to teach society what it means to be a Paralympian, that we're not any different, that we're just like the Olympians, with the same training sites, sponsorships, medals, and venues.* "
>
> —in 2016, to *The New York Times*

FAST FACT:
Lopez won the New Mexico amateur tournament when she was 12 and the U.S. Girls' Junior Championship at 15 and again at 17.

Which golfer was the top rookie and player the same year she had the LPGA tour's lowest scoring average?

In 1978, 21-year-old **Nancy Lopez** announced her arrival to professional golf in grand fashion: She won five straight tournaments and nine total, including the LPGA Championship, and earned the tour's three major honors, still the only player to do so. "That year was a dream come true," she said.

Lopez became a popular star and an ambassador for the struggling LPGA. "She has been to the women's professional golf tour what

Billie Jean King was to women's tennis," wrote SPORTS ILLUSTRATED in 1979, "the individual who, because of her energy and skill, almost single-handedly brought widespread acceptance to a game previously regarded with indifference or contempt."

She was known for being an exceptional athlete and also for being exceptionally kind. After a quarter-century on the LPGA tour, she retired with 48 victories.

Who won the inaugural women's Olympic marathon?

The men's marathon has been included in the Olympics since the first modern Games, in 1896, but it wasn't until nearly a century later that women were granted a 26.2-mile event of their own. At the 1984 Games, **Joan Benoit Samuelson** of Maine was frustrated with the race's early pace and sped ahead of the pack in the first three miles. The other runners waited for her to fade, but she never did. "I took a chance," she said, "and I lucked out." Her time of 2:24:52 earned her gold by nearly 1½ minutes.

Who was the most recent two-time Olympic gold medalist in women's figure skating?

She landed her first triple jump when she was 11 years old and was a world and Olympic champion at 18. **Katarina Witt** skated with skill and grace, dominating the sport during the 1980s. Competing for East Germany, she joined Sonja Henie as the only other woman to ever defend an Olympic singles title (1984, 1988), and Witt won four of the five world championships held during that time. She also won six straight European championships, from 1983 through 1988. Like Henie before her, Witt was also an actress. "But the role I like best is of champion," said Witt.

Which U.S. hockey player has won 13 world championship medals?

You've obviously done a little something special when your hometown celebrates a day in your honor. Indeed, hockey player **Hilary Knight** had won three world championships in four appearances, an NCAA championship at Wisconsin, and a silver Olympic medal when Sun Valley, Idaho, recognized her in 2011. She was a star already, but over the next 12 years, she would become one of the greatest women's hockey players in U.S. history. Knight won six more world championship gold medals and three silvers, and was named MVP of the 2015 and 2016 tournaments. She also scored twice to help Team USA win gold at the 2018 Olympics.

FAST FACT:
Knight holds a handful of Wisconsin career records, including for points (262), goals (143), and game-winning goals (30).

Which soccer player was named FIFA's female athlete of the 20th century?

She scored the first-ever goal for the U.S. women's national team in its first year of existence (1985), and she scored the game-winner in America's first-ever soccer world championship (the 1991 Women's World Cup). The 5'10" **Michelle Akers** was an imposing figure on the field and a figurative giant off it, an integral part of women's soccer's growth. "Our game is fast," she said in 1992. "It's fun. And when more people see women playing soccer at this level, they are going to get hooked." She was right!

Who was the last American to win three straight ladies' world figure skating titles?

Credited with ushering in the modern era of figure skating, **Peggy Fleming** won over America—and everyone else—with her elegance and stylishness on the ice in winning five consecutive U.S. titles starting in 1964, three straight world championships beginning in 1966, and the 1968 Olympic crown. She earned Team USA's only gold of those Games after finishing in sixth place in 1964, and she landed on the covers of LIFE and SPORTS ILLUSTRATED.

Leading up to the 1968 Olympics, her mother, Doris, spent a week furiously sewing six competition outfits from which her daughter could choose. Despite delivering a less-than-perfect routine that left her in tears, Fleming won convincingly over her rivals. "It was all rougher than I thought," she said afterward. "I mean, up until tonight I had figured the worst part of the whole thing came a week ago when I came out to practice. All my competitors came around and sat on the edge of the rink and just killed me with piercing looks. I got through that all right, but this was something else."

> *There are lots of disappointments ... sometimes I fight against being human ... but in overcoming these I learn, and that makes my life worthwhile."*
> —in 1966, to
> SPORTS ILLUSTRATED

WOW FACTOR

15

Fleming's age when she became the youngest U.S. women's figure skating champion.

Who is the first Japanese woman to win a major tennis title?

When she was just four years old, **Naomi Osaka** and her family moved from her native Japan to Long Island, N.Y. In her WTA Tour debut match as a 16-year-old, she defeated a former U.S. Open champion. Then, in 2018, she beat 23-time Grand Slam singles champion Serena Williams to win the U.S. Open herself, the first Japanese player to claim such a prize. Osaka has since won another U.S. Open and two Australian Opens, and has twice been ranked the top woman in the world. Osaka has also made an impact off the court, becoming one of the most marketable athletes in the world and an advocate for numerous causes from racial equality to mental health in sports.

FAST FACT:
Osaka became the first tennis player to light the Olympic cauldron during the opening ceremony at the 2020 Tokyo Olympics.

Who won the most New York City Marathons?

The first time **Grete Waitz** of Norway ever ran a marathon, she broke the world record by more than two minutes (2:32:30). That was at the 1978 New York City Marathon, and Waitz, a world-class runner at 3,000 meters and 10 kilometers, had completed only half of a marathon on her longest training run. It wasn't until after that unexpected New York win that she became serious about running the marathon. At the 1979 event, in fact, she beat her time by nearly five minutes to become the first woman to officially break 2½ hours at the distance (2:27:33). She won New York a record nine times.

Waitz was a role model to younger women in the world of distance running and beloved for her humility.

WOW FACTOR

6

Distances at which Waitz set world records: 3,000 meters, 8K, 10K, 15K, 10 miles, and the marathon.

Who scored the quickest goal in U.S. women's national team history?

WOW FACTOR

121

Goals a 34-year-old Morgan had scored for the USWNT through December 2023, eighth on the all-time list.

Twelve seconds after the whistle blew to begin a U.S. women's national team Olympic qualifier in February 2016, **Alex Morgan** sprinted downfield, corralling a header from teammate Carli Lloyd and powering a kick into the back of the net past a stunned Costa Rica goalkeeper. It was believed to be the fastest goal scored in USWNT history.

Morgan is one of the most popular and accomplished players in U.S. soccer history. She was the youngest player on the USWNT at the 2011 FIFA Women's World Cup, and helped the U.S. win that tournament in 2015 and 2019. At the London Olympics in 2012, she joined Mia Hamm as the only American women to notch 20 goals and 20 assists in a single season. She also co-captained the U.S. squad, with Carli Lloyd and Megan Rapinoe, from 2018 to 2020.

DID YOU KNOW?

In 2015, Morgan and her Portland Thorns teammates Christine Sinclair and Steph Catley became the first women to appear on the cover of EA Sports' latest FIFA video game, *FIFA 16*. The trio graced the covers of the game's region-specific packaging in the U.S., Canada, and Australia, respectively.

Who is the most decorated Olympic tennis player of this century?

ver a 16-year span, **Venus Williams** won an impressive five Olympic medals to tie for most in history among all tennis players. (Kathleen McKane of Great Britain won gold, two silvers, and two bronze in the 1920s.)

She kick-started her Olympic career in 2000 by being the first in 76 years to win singles and doubles at the same Games. Williams, of course, played doubles with sister Serena, and the duo won two more gold medals together.

Though the sisters didn't medal in women's doubles at the 2016 Games, Williams paired with Rajeev Ram, who plays on the ATP Tour, to win silver in mixed doubles and tie the record.

Through 2023, Williams also had seven Grand Slam singles titles.

Who scored gold-medal-winning goals for the U.S. women's soccer team in the 2008 and 2012 Olympics?

Casual soccer fans who tuned into the 2015 Women's World Cup final to see **Carli Lloyd** score a hat trick (three goals) in 16 minutes in Team USA's 5–2 win over Japan thought a star was emerging. The 32-year-old Lloyd's star, however, had been burning bright for quite some time.

This was the same player who had scored the lone goal in a 1–0 overtime win against Brazil in the 2008 Olympic gold medal game and who had scored both goals in a 2–1 win over Japan in the 2012 Olympic gold medal game.

This was also the same Lloyd who was cut from the U.S. Under-21 team and considered quitting the sport. "If you don't have difficult times, you don't learn or break barriers," she said after the 2015 World Cup win. "This journey has taught me so much."

WOW FACTOR

5

Medals Retton won at the 1984 Olympics, more than any athlete there. She took silver in the team event and vault, and bronze in the uneven bars and floor exercise.

Who was the first American woman to win the Olympic all-around?

The best that female U.S. gymnasts had ever fared at the Olympics was to earn bronze in the team event in 1948. Then along came 16-year-old **Mary Lou Retton**, performing in front of a boisterous crowd in Los Angeles at the 1984 Games. She needed to stick her vault, one of her strongest events, in order to win the all-around competition. She stuck it, all right: Retton scored a perfect 10 to clinch a victory, then landed another perfect 10 on her second run (which didn't even matter). "I knew I had it," she said later. "Listen: I knew by my run that I had it. I knew it when I was in the air!"

Along with Edwin Moses, America's 400-meter hurdler extraordinaire, Retton was named SPORTS ILLUSTRATED Sportsperson of the Year. "Well, nobody thought it could be done," she said of winning gold. "But you know what? I went and did it."

DID YOU KNOW?

After her big win in 1984, Retton became the first woman to appear on the front of Wheaties cereal boxes, which had for decades featured men. She rode in the Macy's Thanksgiving Day parade and appeared on the cover of *Seventeen* magazine—she was everywhere. America adored her. "I still think it's kind of neat," she said later that year of her instant fame. "I mean, I'd understand people recognizing me if I had purple hair or something, but I'm just a normal teenager. I'm still just Mary Lou."

DID YOU KNOW?

Nurse's family is filled with professional athletes. Her uncle, Donovan McNabb, starred at quarterback for the Philadelphia Eagles. Her cousins include two-time Olympian and WNBA All-Star Kia Nurse and Edmonton Oilers defenseman Darnell Nurse.

Which hockey player holds the record for most goals and assists in a single Olympics?

Canadian hockey player **Sarah Nurse** is a big star; after all, she'd had a Barbie doll made in her likeness in 2020, and was featured on a Cheerios cereal box in 2022. But her performance at the Beijing Olympics lifted her into the stratosphere and made her one of the biggest stars in women's hockey. Nurse set two new Olympic records, for most points (18) and most assists (13) in a single women's tournament as Canada claimed the gold medal after beating the United States 3–2 in the final. She also played a role in the launch of the Professional Women's Hockey League and currently plays for Toronto.

FAST FACT:
Lawrence skied down a mountain with the Olympic flame during the opening ceremony of the 1960 Games in Squaw Valley, California.

Who is the only American skier to win two golds in a single Olympics?

nly 15 when she competed at the 1948 Olympics, **Andrea Mead Lawrence** finished eighth in the slalom, 21st in the combined event, and 35th in the downhill. She went on to win 10 of 16 races in 1951, including the event that served as an unofficial world championship. Lawrence arrived in Oslo, Norway, for the 1952 Games as the team captain, focused and determined. She hiked up and down the 1,000-meter giant slalom course, making mental notes about adjustments she should try. She won by more than two seconds, finishing in 2:06.8. ("Gee,

that's good," she said afterward. "I didn't think I was going that fast.")

She fell twice during the downhill and didn't medal, and she took a tumble on her first slalom run. But she got back up and was in fourth place heading into the second and final run. She turned in the fastest time of the day by two seconds to win slalom gold by eight-tenths of a second.

Later in life, she became a conservationist, founding environmental organizations such as the Andrea Lawrence Institute for Mountains and Rivers.

Who was named top Canadian female athlete of the 20th century?

Nicknamed Tiger by her teammates for the tenacious way she tackled the slopes, **Nancy Greene** of British Columbia won the inaugural Alpine skiing World Cup, in 1967. She then earned silver in the slalom and gold in the giant slalom at the 1968 Olympics, winning the latter race by a record margin (2.68 seconds). She repeated as overall World Cup champion in 1968, and by the time she retired, she had 17 Canadian national titles as well. In November 1999, she was named the Canadian female athlete of the century for her accomplishments as a competitor and as an advocate for her sport. She was appointed to the Canadian Senate in 2009.

Who won five consecutive world figure skating titles in the 1950s?

For three years, **Carol Heiss** of New York battled countrywoman Tenley Albright for the title of best in the U.S. and the world. Heiss finished second to Albright at three straight national championships, at the 1955 world championships, and at the 1956 Olympics. One month after those Games, however, Heiss prevailed at worlds, the first of five in a row at which she would win gold. (The next month Heiss lost the U.S. title to Albright but then won four in a row.)

The spotlight was all Heiss's at the 1960 Games, where the 20-year-old New York University junior won gold. A ticker-tape parade was held in New York City in her honor.

Who was named MVP in four straight WNBA Finals?

She was playing overseas when **Cynthia Cooper-Dyke** heard about a new league starting in the U.S., the WNBA. Already 34 years old when she joined the Houston Comets during the summer of 1997, she teamed up with Sheryl Swoopes and Tina Thompson to lead the franchise to the league's first four titles, winning Finals MVP each time. Cooper-Dyke was also named league MVP in 1997 and 1998, the only time (through 2023) that a player has won the award in back-to-back years. She retired after winning that fourth championship, in 2000, then returned to the WNBA for a brief stint at age 40. Cooper-Dyke was inducted into the Hall of Fame in 2010.

PLAYER INDEX

PHOTO CREDITS